❄ GREAT CHRISTMAS ❄
Ornament and Stocking Ideas

❄ GREAT CHRISTMAS ❄
Ornament and Stocking Ideas

Carol Endler Sterbenz • Photography by Bill Milne

CRESCENT BOOKS
NEW YORK ● AVENEL, NEW JERSEY

A FRIEDMAN GROUP BOOK

This 1994 edition published by Crescent Books, distributed by Outlet Book Company, Inc., a
Random House Company,
40 Engelhard Avenue, Avenel, New Jersey 07001.

Random House
New York ● Toronto ● London ● Sydney ● Auckland

ISBN 0-517-10304-4

SIMPLY SENSATIONAL:
GREAT CHRISTMAS ORNAMENT AND STOCKING IDEAS
was prepared and produced by
Michael Friedman Publishing Group, Inc.
15 West 26th Street
New York, New York 10010

Editor: Elizabeth Viscott Sullivan
Designer: Lynne Yeamans
Art Director: Jeff Batzli
Photography Editor: Christopher C. Bain
Editorial Consultant: Eleanor Levie

Color separations by Rainbow Graphic Arts Co., Ltd.
Printed and bound in China by Leefung-Asco Printers Ltd.

8 7 6 5 4 3 2 1

Every effort has been made to present the information in this book in a clear, complete, and accurate
manner. It is important that all instructions be carefully followed, as failure to do so could result in in-
jury, and the publisher and the author expressly disclaim any and all liability resulting therefrom.

To the Bombers, with love

Acknowledgments

❁ ❁ ❁

I would like to thank the following colleagues and friends who worked closely with me on this project: Elizabeth Sullivan, Lynne Yeamans, and Christopher Bain of the Michael Friedman Publishing Group; Eleanor Levie; Bill Milne and Barb Norman; Mary Ann Hurd of Baycrest Antiques and Design, Huntington, New York; Just Accents, at the Vayban Showroom in New York City.

As always, I would like to thank my family for their love and support.

C.E.S.

CONTENTS

Introduction

Few traditions connect us to past Christmases more than the custom of decorating a tree, a custom that began in northern Europe in the fifteenth century as part of the staging of miracle plays. It is thought that the first "Christmas tree" may have been the Paradise Tree, a theatrical prop used to explain the story of Adam and Eve in the Garden of Eden. This tree was adorned sparingly—shiny red apples and cherries and white communion wafers were its only decorations. Although miracle plays were eventually banned, the custom of decorating a tree at Christmas was adopted by many families living in northern Europe, particularly those living in the regions that now comprise France and Germany.

The tradition of decorating Christmas trees quickly spread to other European countries and, as it did, ornamentation became more varied and elaborate. Candles, pine cones, small gifts, pastries, and gilded nuts were commonly used adornments. When Queen Victoria and Prince Albert adopted the tree-decorating tradition in England in 1848, they added a multitude of miniature toys and animals, as well as baskets and paper cornucopias filled with all sorts of candy and fruit.

Introduction

The custom of tree trimming and decorating the home at Christmas reached North America in the seventeenth century, when the Germans immigrated to Pennsylvania. Reflecting a simpler way of life and a closeness to the land and its bounty, the Pennsylvania Deutsch (later known as the Pennsylvania Dutch) produced carved wooden figures, dried fruit, cookies, and strands of berries and popcorn at Yuletime. Pioneers continued the tradition on the American frontier, making ornaments with ingenuity, as they used whatever was on hand to create a sense of home and celebration.

The projects in Great Christmas Ornament and Stocking Ideas were inspired by the styles of these two great historical eras: Victorian England and late-nineteenth-century America. Each period has a distinct and beautiful style of ornamentation that is still popular today.

This book is meant to inspire you to take part in the much-beloved and time-honored tradition of ornament making. All of the projects included here are easy, quick, and a lot of fun to create, making them suitable for beginning and experienced crafters alike. And best of all, whether hung on a tree or used to adorn a mantel or a table, or to add a special touch to gift packages, these handcrafted ornaments possess charm that will make them a cherished part of Christmas for years to come.

The Victoriana Collection

Although Victorian Christmas trees were small enough to be placed on tabletops, they were symbols of elegance and abundance. Each branch was laden with miniature baskets of candy, tiny dried-flower wreaths, and a great variety of penny toys and toy animals. No tree was complete without a miniature steam train or paper ornaments made from Christmas cards. Early on Christmas day, piles of unwrapped gifts were placed on the damask-draped tabletop with the tree.

You can celebrate the holiday season in a nineteenth-century fashion by adorning your tree with handmade versions of traditional Victorian ornaments. The techniques are simple, and because the items are small, the amounts and cost of lavish materials such as velvet, gold trim, ribbon, and lace are minimal. Antique prints add a charming touch and are available in reproduction form. Die-cut prints or stickers with nostalgic cherubs and angels, available at your local card or stationery store, are nice additions, too. With the addition of a few elegant details, your designs will evoke the days of a splendid, romantic, old-fashioned Christmas.

Treetop Angel

❀ ❀ ❀

Trimming the tree just wouldn't be complete without this Victorian ornament, just 7" high. While she's lavishly embellished with trimmings, this angel is an easy, no-sew project.

MATERIALS:

* Lightweight cardboard
* Old-fashioned print of a child's or young woman's face
* Polyester fiberfill
* Ecru moiré fabric
* 1³/₄ yards 4"-wide scallop-edge ecru lace
* 2 large gold fabric leaves
* 2-yard string gold beads
* 2 yards gold picot-edge trim
* ¹/₄ yard thick gold twisted cord
* 1 yard ¹/₄"-wide gold braid trim
* 30 small ribbon roses in assorted pastel colors
* 3mm gold bead
* Fabric glue
* Hot-glue gun and hot-melt glue sticks
* Pencil, paper, compass, masking tape, and scissors

DIRECTIONS:

Read Using a Hot-Glue Gun on page 61 and follow the directions for Making a Cardboard Cone on page 62. Back the print of the face with cardboard, cut it out and, inserting a bit of fiberfill underneath, glue it to the inverted cone, close to the tip.

Cut rectangles from the moiré: one 7"×28" and one 5"×8". For the hood, fold the smaller rectangle lengthwise, slightly off-center, then fold it over and use the fabric glue to affix the long extending edge on top, like an envelope flap (refer to the diagram on page 13).

Turn the rectangle over and glue the picot-edge trim lengthwise along the center, then turn the rectangle back and over again. Referring to the dash lines in the diagram, fold the top corners down to bring the left and right sides of the flap edge together. Overlap the edges slightly, then secure them with glue.

Treetop Angel

Lightly stuff the peak that is formed with fiberfill, then glue the hood over the cone and face. Hot-glue the edges of the hood, loosely gathered or pleated, in place around the face and neck.

For the cape, use the large rectangle. Press the long edges under 1/4", and one short edge under 1"; use fabric glue to secure them. Glue the picot-edge trim along the short folded edge, continuing along the long edge to within 2" from the opposite short edge, then across the rectangle 2" from that short edge. Pinching small pleats as you work, hot-glue this rectangle around the neck so that the trimmed side edges are both below the angel's face.

Lift up the cape and glue 1 yard of lace, generously gathered into pleats, around the cardboard cone so that 1/2" of the lace shows beyond the cone and cape. Cut the remaining lace in half and form each half into a ring, gluing to secure. Flatten these rings and glue them to the back of the angel, pinching, pleating, and gathering them at their crosswise and lengthwise centers to form wings. Glue a fabric leaf over each wing.

Hot-glue one end of the gold twisted cord between the back of the hood and the left wing. Guide the cord in a large S curve over the front of the cape, hot-gluing the bottom half to the cape. Hot-glue ribbon roses all along the curve. Weave strings of gold beads around the hood, the cord, and the ribbon roses, making loops and curls, and letting the ends trail. Glue a few ribbon roses to the gold beads.

Tie a small bow at the center of the gold braid trim and glue it under the face. Accent the bow knot with a gold bead and let the streamer ends cascade downward.

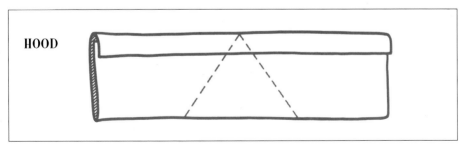

HOOD

Cherubs

✽ ✽ ✽

*Cherubs, 3¹/2" high, are the
subject here, but identical images of
any figure or item that suggests
a three-dimensional quality would
be appropriate. Consider, for
example, fruit, kittens, puppies,
or old-fashioned toys.*

MATERIALS FOR EACH:

* 6 identical nostalgic prints of figure or object
* Matte-finish water-base varnish or sealer
* Seed pearls and seed beads
* Curved cuticle scissors
* Hot-glue gun and hot-melt glue sticks

Optional:

* ³/4 yard ¹/8"-wide satin ribbon in matching color
* Ribbon roses in desired colors

DIRECTIONS:

Carefully cut out each of the six prints. Consider which areas seem to come forward toward the viewer, which parts suggest layers or roundness, and which elements deserve extra attention. (On the cherub, for example, the drape of fabric and one arm seem closest to the viewer; the wing seems layered; the arms, legs, and head seem rounded; the face is the major focus of attention.) These are the areas that you will "pad" or mound up with hot glue.

Read Using a Hot-Glue Gun on page 61. Begin by laying one print on the work surface, then apply a drop or a stream of hot glue onto those areas that you wish to build up. Let the glue dry, then apply tiny dots of glue all over the print, and gently press a second print on top.

For a hanging loop, use a pin to pierce the two layers near the top of the ornament; insert a short length of wire through the hole. Thread on beads, then twist the wire ends together. Conceal the wire ends with successive layers of hot glue and paper.

On the remaining prints, cut out only the specific areas you wish to emphasize (in this case, the head, wings, arm, fabric drape, legs, and a predominant flower). Add them to the main print in layers, mounding the

Cherubs and Cornucopia

hot glue in between and curving, folding, or shaping the pieces as necessary. Paint the entire ornament with a generous coat of varnish, sealing all the surfaces and edges and filling in the spaces between layers.

Embellish the finished ornament with ribbon roses and a cascade of ribbon.

Cornucopia

❋ ❋ ❋

Like the Victorians, you'll want to fill this cone-shaped paper container (5¹/₂" tall) with nuts, candy, coins, or tiny wrapped packages.

MATERIALS:

* Lightweight cardboard
* Wrapping paper with an ornate pattern
* Spray adhesive
* 3 yards gold cord
* Ribbon roses
* Fine-gauge wire
* Large pearl bead and pearl seed beads
* 1 yard 1¹/₂"-wide wire-edge ribbon
* Hot-glue gun and hot-melt glue sticks
* Pencil, paper, scissors, compass, and masking tape
* Stapler

DIRECTIONS:

Read Using a Hot-Glue Gun and Making a Cardboard Cone on pages 61 and 62. Make a cardboard cone covered with wrapping paper.

Trim ¹/₄" from the top edge of the covered cone. For a ruffle, gather one edge of the ribbon tightly, either by pulling on wire or by sewing a small running stitch and pulling the thread ends. Glue the ruffle to the top of the cone, along the inside.

For a handle, cut an 8" length from gold cord. Staple the ends of the cord to opposite sides of the cone, on the inside. Apply hot glue a little at a time and carefully arrange the remaining gold cord around the cone in one continuous length: first along the rim, then in small loops and in deep scallops just below the rim, and finally snaking and curling toward the tip.

Make ten ringlets of wire, each strung with eight seed beads. Place one ringlet over the tip of the cone, with a large pearl bead glued at the point. Hot-glue one ringlet between each scallop of cord. Hot-glue ribbon roses along the snaking cord.

Candy Pouches

❈ ❈ ❈

Embellish a two-dimensional ornament by attaching a gossamer sack of little candies or small keepsakes. This ornament is about 3"×8".

MATERIALS:

* Die-cut cardboard angel, or other image, printed on both sides
* 1/4 yard narrow gold picot-edge trim (for angel's halo)
* Gold mesh candy bag or small amount of gold tulle
* Gold thread
* Small packages 3–5mm gold beads, one each bugle and barrel

* Beading needle
* Hot-glue gun and hot-melt glue sticks

DIRECTIONS:

Read Using a Hot-Glue Gun on page 61. To form a halo for the angel ornament, cut two 2" lengths of picot-edge trim. Turn the ends 1/4" to the wrong side and hot-glue them above the head.

To make a mesh pouch, cut a circle with a 6" radius from the tulle. Turn the edges 3/4" to the wrong side and stitch 1/2" from the fold all around; pull the thread ends to gather the circle into a pouch.

Fill the sack with treats. Fit the sack over the bottom of the ornament, gluing as needed to secure it in place. Pull the thread ends tight to close the pouch; tie the ends in a neat bow.

To decorate the bottom of the pouch with beaded loops, thread a needle and backstitch a few times over the bottom center of the pouch. Insert the needle through eight bugle beads and then through a backstitch: repeat this eleven times more; every other time add one more bugle bead to the count to obtain progressively longer loops. Finish decorating the pouch with two 2" strings (*not* loops) of barrel beads.

Tussie-Mussie

❋ ❋ ❋

A tussie-mussie is an old-fashioned aromatic bouquet, and this one, 9" high, is quite a Victorian fantasy. Spray the arrangement with cologne or mix potpourri in with the flowers.

MATERIALS:

* Gold wrapping paper
* Lightweight cardboard
* 1/2 yard 3"-wide ecru lace
* Dry floral foam
* Assortment of dried florals such as tea roses, cockscomb, statice, pepper berries, and caspia
* Small artificial fruits such as berries, grapes, and prune plums
* Ultrafine gold glitter
* Gold cord
* Hot-glue gun and hot-melt glue sticks
* Spray adhesive
* Compass, paper, pencil, scissors, and masking tape

DIRECTIONS:

Read Using a Hot-Glue Gun, Arranging Floral Materials, and Making a Cardboard Cone on pages 61 and 62. Follow the instructions given there to make a giftwrap-covered cardboard cone.

Hot-glue short sections of lace around the inside edge of the rim of the cone, gathering lace as you work. Hot-glue a large chunk of dry foam into the cone and trim it only slightly to create a large rounded mound that extends well past the rim.

Hot-glue dried florals and artificial fruits all around this mound. Start with the largest pieces and work down to the smallest, but work with one type of floral material at a time and distribute it evenly.

For flowers, trim the stems to 1", then press them into the foam, making sure the flower heads are secured so that they radiate outward. Separate the artificial berries or grapes into individual units. Overlap the flowers and berries for a lush, dense effect.

Spray the florals with adhesive and dust them with glitter. Set the tussie-mussie on a shelf, mantel, or tabletop, and swirl gold cord over the cone.

Candy Pouches and Tussie-Mussie

Floral Heart

Floral Heart

❋ ❋ ❋

*This symbol of love and giving is
romantically interpreted here
in tea roses and shimmering berries.
Choose any dried florals for
this 5¹/2" decoration, which is versatile
enough to adorn a mantel, tree,
table, nook, or wall.*

MATERIALS:

* Medium-gauge wire
* Floral tape
* ¹/4 yard thick gold twisted cord
* Dried florals: 18 tea roses, small bunch
  of statice, delphinium stem, hydrangea
  blossom, juniper or other small-scale
  evergreen, sprig of pepper berries
* Cluster of artificial berries or grapes
* Spray adhesive
* Fine glitter or iridescent crystals
* Hot-glue gun and hot-melt glue sticks
* Wire cutters

DIRECTIONS:

Read Using a Hot-Glue Gun and Arranging
Floral Materials on page 61. Cut a 10" length
of wire and bend it into a heart shape, twisting the ends together at the bottom. Wrap
the wire heart with floral tape. To hang the
wreath (optional), loop the gold cord into a
pretzel shape, and hot-glue it to the heart so
that it extends above the top at the center.

Place the wreath form, gold loops facing
down, on a protected work surface. Hot-glue
dried florals around the side and front edges
of the wreath form. Start with the largest
blossoms and work down to the smallest, but
work with one type of floral at a time and
distribute it evenly.

For flowers, trim stems to 1", then
arrange the flower heads so that they radiate
outward in various directions.

Separate the artificial berries or grapes
into individual units. Spray them with adhesive, dust them with glitter, and hot-glue
them, evenly spaced, into any empty areas.

Hobby Horses

✱ ✱ ✱

Hobby horses were a staple toy of the Victorian nursery. Stitch up several of these steeds, 6³/4" high, in colors to match your decor or to present to holiday guests.

MATERIALS FOR EACH:

* Small amounts of cotton fabric in 3 coordinating solids and prints
* Sewing thread to match fabric
* ³/8"-diameter wood dowel, cut to a 4¹/2" length
* Two ³/8" buttons
* ¹/4 yard satin cord
* ¹/4 yard contrasting ribbon
* 2 large sequins
* Polyester fiberfill
* Clear nylon thread

* Tacky glue
* Sewing needle and pins
* Pencil, tracing paper, scissors
* Hot-glue gun and hot-melt glue sticks

DIRECTIONS:

Read Using a Hot-Glue Gun and Sewing on pages 61 and 63. Trace the actual-size patterns (page 65) for the hobby-horse head and ear; use these to cut out two of each from the same fabric.

From a third fabric, cut nine strips 1¹/2"×2¹/2". From a fourth fabric, cut one strip 1"×12¹/2". On each strip, press the long edges ¹/4" to the wrong side, then fold the strip lengthwise in half (wrong side in), and stitch it close to the edge through all of the layers. Press.

For a mane, fold the short strips made from the third fabric crosswise in half. Pin them snugly side by side along the top and back, with raw edges matching. Detach the strip closest to the muzzle and trim it to a 1" length; refold it and pin it back into its original position.

Place the second head piece on top of the first, and sew around all but the straight bottom edge. Clip seam allowances and turn

Hobby Horses

the head to the right side. Stuff the head firmly with fiberfill to within ¹/₂" of the raw edge. Sew gathering stitches around the bottom edge.

Using the tacky glue, affix the satin cord in a spiral along the dowel stick. Insert one end of the dowel into the bottom of the head. Apply hot glue, then immediately pull the gathering stitches tight. Push the horse's head down over the dowel so that the raw edges are pushed to the inside. Hold the head and the dowel until the glue bonds.

Sew a button "eye" to either side of the head. On each ear piece, turn the straight edge under ¹/₄". Stitch the curved edge under and gather the stitches. Fold the ear piece in half and tack each ear in place.

For reins, use the narrow strip made from the fourth fabric to wrap the muzzle and make a loop under the head, tacking as needed. Embellish the rein with a scrap of notched ribbon and sequins.

Guide nylon thread through a loop of the mane to make a hanging loop.

Nostalgic Diorama

❆ ❆ ❆

The oval shape of this 2³/₄" × 3³/₈" box is reminiscent of Fabergé eggs, which often reveal detailed miniature scenes. Look through magazines or catalogs, or use old Christmas cards for a suitable background print for this seasonal diorama.

MATERIALS:

* Small oval chipwood box
* Small print or depiction of a winter landscape
* Miniature train (available in craft stores and often sold as a cake decoration in card and party stores)
* Acrylic paints in assorted colors
* 2 or 3 very slender twigs
* A dried leaf or sprig that suggests a tree shape (here, dusty miller)

* 3/8 yard 11/2"-wide ribbon
* 3/8 yard 3/8"-wide gold picot-edge trim
* Batting
* Fine gold thread
* Small cluster of artificial berries
* Sprig of boxwood leaves
* Ribbon rose
* Fine tapered paintbrushes
* Hot-glue gun and hot-melt glue sticks
* Tacky glue, scissors, and pencil
* Sharp embroidery needle

DIRECTIONS:

Read Using a Hot-Glue Gun on page 61. Place the box horizontally over the printed scene and trace around it. Cut out the oval and glue it to the inside bottom of the box. If significant pieces of the scene remain, you may wish to glue them around the inside of the box.

Cut a small rectangle of batting and glue it to the box for a snowy ground. Break pieces of twig to fit across the box on the inside to naturally "curtain" the scene; hot-glue the twig ends to secure them. Glue a leaf or two beside the twigs. Use the paintbrush to add details and decorative motifs to the miniature train, then hot-glue the train in the foreground.

Spread tacky glue around the box, then wrap it with ribbon. At the rim edge of the box, trim excess ribbon and hot-glue picot-edge trim all around.

Use a sharp needle to pierce a small hole in the center top of the diorama and to guide the ends of a loop of gold thread to the inside. Remove the needle and knot the thread ends to secure. Hot-glue boxwood, berries, and a ribbon rose to the center top of the ornament.

Berry Wreath
❈ ❈ ❈

If you can't find sprigs of dried tallowberry (small white berry clusters), substitute small artificial berries or even popcorn for this 3" ornament.

MATERIALS:

* Very slender twigs or vines
* Fine-gauge wire

(materials list continues on page 27)

Nostalgic Diorama and Berry Wreath

* A few sprigs of dried white tallowberry
* Dried red rosebud
* Small bunches of artificial berries, 1/8"–3/8" in diameter: an assortment of bright, dark, and metallic reds
* Sprigs of boxwood
* 1/2 yard red 1/2"-wide ribbon
* Hot-glue gun and hot-melt glue sticks

DIRECTIONS:

Read Using a Hot-Glue Gun and Making a Vine Wreath on pages 61 and 62.

Make a wreath 3" in diameter and 1/2" thick. To make a hanging loop, weave a 4" strand of wire through a few twigs on the back and twist the ends together.

Hot-glue florals, one type at a time, all around the wreath. First, break boxwood sprigs into small pieces and glue them on so they radiate outward. Next, add clusters of tallowberry or other white berries all around. Add a rosebud and a ribbon bow as shown in the photograph. Intersperse red berries among the white berries along only the bottom half of the wreath.

Seed Pod Wreath

❊ ❊ ❊

Take a walk through the woods, a park, or along a country road and you'll find most of the makings for this 3" wreath.

MATERIALS:

* Slender twigs (here, birch) or vines
* Fine-gauge wire
* Tiny pine cones, seed pods, burrs, and acorns
* Non-dyed small-scale dried flowers: everlastings, white cockscomb, wheat
* Heavy clear monofilament
* Gold 3mm beads
* Tiny gold bell
* Antique gold metallic wax finish or gold paint and paintbrush
* 1 1/2 yards 1/4"-wide gold braid trim
* Hot-glue gun and hot-melt glue sticks

Seed Pod Wreath

DIRECTIONS:

Read Using a Hot-Glue Gun, Arranging Floral Materials, and Making a Vine Wreath on pages 61 and 62. Follow the instructions to make a vine or twig wreath 3" in diameter and 1/2" thick. Gild pine cones and acorn caps by applying wax finish with your finger or by painting them.

Divide the gold braid into thirds. Tie one strand to the wreath for a hanging loop. Tie a small bow in the center of each remaining strand, and, imagining the wreath as a clock face, hot-glue the bow knots to the wreath at the four o'clock point. Loop the streamer ends along the wreath, gluing to secure them.

Create a crescent-shaped spray with the bows at its center. Start by gluing the largest natural items above and below the bows. Working with one type of item at a time, glue the cones, pods, burrs, acorns, the ends of short-stemmed dried flowers, and 1 1/2" lengths of monofilament so that all items radiate outward from the bows along the crescent.

To finish the ornament, glue three gold beads, evenly spaced, along each monofilament strand. Glue on a bell to accent the center of the spray.

Menagerie

❀ ❀ ❀

The members of this small zoo (up to 3 1/2" tall or long) stand on their own, but holes for hanging loops enable them to take up places on your tree, too.

MATERIALS:

* Papier-mâché mix
* Matte-finish water-base varnish or sealer
* Acrylic paint in white and assorted colors
* White six-strand embroidery floss
* Red metallic cord
* Pencil, scissors, tracing paper
* Rolling pin
* Cellophane wrap
* Cookie sheet
* Craft knife #1
* Small blunt knitting, darning, or tapestry needle
* Small flat and fine tapered paintbrushes
* Hot-glue gun and hot-melt glue sticks

DIRECTIONS:

Read Using a Hot-Glue Gun and Papier-Mâché on pages 61 and 62. Prepare the papier-mâché and roll it out to about a 3/16" thickness. You will need about an 8" circle for the animals, and you will prepare another small batch for the stands later on.

Trace and cut out the actual-size patterns (pages 66 and 67) for each animal. Cut out separate ears for the elephant. For all of the other animals, roll up bits of papier-mâché the size of a small pea, and using a blunt needle, shape each one into a hollow semi-sphere. Using a little extra moisture, gently pinch and press the ears onto each animal as shown in the photograph.

Referring again to the actual-size patterns, use a blunt needle to pierce a small hole at the top center of each ornament for an optional hanging loop and to sculpt some details, as shown on the patterns with heavy inside lines. Be sure to let the shapes dry fully; overnight is best.

For stands, mix and roll out a similar batch of papier-mâché, and cut it into 1"-wide strips. Gently press each hardened animal onto a strip, with its feet centered along the width and sinking slightly into the papier-mâché. Trim the stand so it extends only 1/4" past the animal. Let the stand dry, then varnish the entire ornament.

To paint, add a little white paint to each color for a sherbet-toned pastel. Paint a base coat on each side, letting the paint dry after each coat. Use a fine tapered brush and a contrast color to paint on a pattern of squiggles or triangles. With a quick, up-and-down motion, scatter white polka dots. Add stripes along the edges. Dot the eye with a darker color. Let the paint dry, then repeat the pattern on the reverse side.

Hot-glue a red bow to each head and a 1" length of knotted six-strand floss to the rumps of all but the chimp, for tails. If desired, insert a 5" length of floss through the hole to make a hanging loop.

Menagerie

The Country Collection

The country look will never go out of fashion. Basic lines, homespun textures, and natural materials combine to create a style that is straightforward and uncomplicated. As country suggests home, hearth, and family history, it is a look that is warm and inviting. And at no other time is the hand-crafted, charming spirit of "country" more welcome than at Christmas. The materials needed for most of the designs in the Country Collection are yours for the picking. You need go no farther than your own backyard, local park, or woods to find twigs and pine cones. Your kitchen pantry probably holds most of the necessary ingredients for the Gingerbread Birdhouses. And scraps of fabric are all you need to make the easy piecework projects.

In the tradition of handcrafting, no two pieces come out exactly alike. Country style, with its informal invitation to try your hand at something, also prompts you to interpret and personalize any design. A change in color or pattern, or additional detail will not diminish the value of the design, but elevate it as a unique piece of folk art.

❄

Indulge your own creativity in the spirit of the season! By making, enjoying, and giving your own handmade ornaments, you'll learn the joys of a country Christmas…no matter where you live.

Folk-Art Swag

❀ ❀ ❀

The heart, the star, and the heart-in-hand motifs are nostalgic and contemporary symbols of faith and love. Make them with your own cookie cutters or use the 2"-3" patterns given.

MATERIALS:

* Papier-mâché mix
* Matte-finish water-base varnish or sealer
* Red and metallic gold acrylic paint
* Red and gold seed beads
* Fine-gauge brass-finish wire
* Pencil, tracing paper, scissors, and craft knife #1 or small heart and star cookie cutters
* Spatula
* Rolling pin
* Cellophane wrap
* Cookie sheet
* Small blunt knitting, darning, or tapestry needle
* Small flat paintbrushes

For a swag:
* Red satin and gold metallic twisted cord

DIRECTIONS:

Read Papier-Mâché on page 62. Prepare the papier-mâché, rolling it out to about a 3/8" thickness.

If you have cookie cutters, use them to cut out shapes. Otherwise, trace and cut out the actual-size patterns (page 68) for each motif; use the patterns to cut out motifs as desired.

For the heart-in-hand ornament, cut out the heart and hand separately. Moisten the back of the heart and lightly press it onto the hand. With a needle, lightly carve lines to show a slight separation between each of the fingers.

On all motifs, use the needle to pierce holes for hanging, either at the center top, for individual ornaments, or at each side, for securing ornaments along a swag. Let the shapes dry.

Folk-Art Swag

Paint the stars and the hand gold, the hearts red. Work first on one side, then on the other, attending to the edges as well. Let the paint dry, then recoat the shapes as necessary. Varnish or otherwise seal them.

To hang the ornaments, thread three seed beads in a matching color onto a 6" length of wire. Slide the beads to the center of the wire, then twist the wire to secure the beads. Insert the wire ends through a hole on the ornament, twist again, separate the wire ends and, leaving a space, twist the ends again with two or three tight turns.

For a swag, pass the cord through the space on the wire. Tighten the wire so the ornaments won't slide across the cord.

Twig Chairs

❅ ❅ ❅

These rustic miniature chairs (5" tall) with their tiny quilt and pillow invite you to indulge in peaceful thoughts of Christmas in the country.

MATERIALS:

* Very slender twigs (here, birch), 1/32"–1/8" thick
* Fine-gauge wire
* 2 tiny pine cones
* Hot-glue gun and hot-melt glue sticks
* Kitchen shears

For miniature quilt and pillow:

* Small amounts of 3 contrasting cotton print fabrics
* Sewing thread to match fabrics
* Very small amount of polyester fiberfill
* Pencil
* Sewing needle and pins

DIRECTIONS:

Read Using a Hot-Glue Gun and Making a Vine Wreath on pages 61 and 62. For a seat frame, wire four 2 1/4"-long twigs into a square. Cut about twelve 2 1/2"-long twigs, and hot-glue them side by side across the seat frame. For legs, cut four 1 1/2"-long heavier twigs and glue them to each corner of the seat frame. For a seat back, choose two twigs that fork off at an angle; position them from the back legs upward so that the angled off-shoots intersect at the top center.

Create curves with the thinnest twigs. If you find that the twigs are dry and too brittle to bend, soak them for a few minutes in a pan of water, then use them to make an oval vine or twig wreath, 2"×2 1/4". Carefully wire the wreath at the join to the center back of the seat.

For chair arms, bend 6" lengths of twigs into a curve that goes from the front legs over to the back legs. Securely wire four of these curved pieces just under the seat and at the bottom of each chair leg.

Refer to the photograph to decorate the chair back and arms with twigs that form inverted Vs; hot-glue two pine cones at the top intersection of twigs.

For a miniature quilt, refer to Sewing on page 63 and to the directions for the Teddy Bear Quilts on page 50. Make a one-patch design, using four square patches from each of two fabrics. From a third fabric, cut four 2"×4 1/2" strips and add these as borders. Omitting batting, add a backing.

For a pillow, cut two 2 1/2" squares from the same fabric used for the quilt border. Pin the squares together and stitch around three sides. Trim the corners and turn the pillow to the right side. Insert a tiny bit of fiberfill, then turn the open edges to the inside and stitch them closed.

Drape the pillow and the quilt over the twig chair, then hot-glue them into place.

Twig Chairs

Miniature Fruit Tree

Miniature Fruit Tree

❋ ❋ ❋

You don't need a green thumb to create this 9¹/₂" tall topiary standard. If you like, you can decorate the tree for Christmas with tiny sequin stars, ribbon roses, bows, or shiny balls.

MATERIALS:

* Terra-cotta flower pot, 2¹/₄" in diameter and 2¹/₄" tall
* Sprigs of boxwood
* Small chunks of dry floral foam
* Small amount of sphagnum moss
* Cluster of artificial grapes or berries
* Small branch
* Green spray paint
* White and gray acrylic paint
* 1 yard ⁷/₈"-wide copper wire-edge ribbon
* Hot-glue gun and hot-melt glue sticks
* Scissors
* Household sponge
* Paper

DIRECTIONS:

Give the flower pot a "time-worn" look by lightly sponging a few areas under the rim with a little gray and white paint, barely blended. Let the paint dry.

Read Using a Hot-Glue Gun on page 61. Cut a chunk of foam that is slightly larger than the flower pot. Apply some hot glue to the bottom of the pot, then gently push in the foam, allowing the foam to extend past the rim of the pot by ¹/₂". Cut the branch to a 5¹/₂" length. Hot-glue and press one end into the center of the foam in the pot, and the other end into a larger chunk of foam. Shape the foam below into a mound around the branch. Apply hot glue to the mound and carefully cover it with sphagnum moss. Shape the foam above the moss into an approximate sphere.

Trim the boxwood into small sprigs. Insert the woody ends of the sprigs into the sphere of foam. Continue until the foam is densely covered. Prune the tree into a neat spherical shape, about 5¹/₂" in diameter. Make a paper collar to temporarily mask the branch and pot, then spray-paint the box-wood. Be sure to let the paint dry before removing the collar.

Separate grapes or berries, then insert their wires into the foam, or hot-glue them between boxwood sprigs. Space the grapes evenly all around the sphere.

Wrap ribbon around the base of the branch and tie a pretty bow. Let the streamer ends cascade gracefully.

Gingerbread Birdhouses

❀ ❀ ❀

Nestle these (3¹/₂" high) little houses amid fresh balsam and pine for a delightful and fragrant tablescape.

MATERIALS:

* Gingerbread dough (see page 42)
* Tube of white decorator icing
* Graph paper (for patterns)
* Wax paper
* Craft knife #1 or paring knife
* Thin wood skewers (for perches)
* Tiny pine cones and feathers (optional, for bird)
* Rolling pin
* Apple corer

DIRECTIONS:

Make the gingerbread dough according to the recipe. While the dough is being refrigerated, mark patterns for each section of the birdhouse on graph paper, following the diagrams on page 42, and cut out the patterns.

Roll out the refrigerated dough to ¹/₄" thickness between sheets of wax paper. Using the patterns, cut around each section with a knife: cut one base, two roof pieces, a front and a back, and two sides. If you wish, cut thirty-two rectangles, ³/₈"×³/₄", for shingles, and similar-sized rectangles for shutters, steps, chimneys, or any other architectural details you wish to add. On the front piece, use an apple corer to cut out a round opening, and press in a short length of skewer, for a perch. Bake and cool the gingerbread pieces according to the recipe.

To construct the birdhouse, position all gingerbread sections on a work surface

Gingerbread Birdhouses

covered with wax paper. Cement pieces together with icing as follows: attach the sides along their edges to the front piece, then put on the back piece. Cement all four walls to the base, with a front "porch" extending slightly more than the other sides. Center each roof piece over the angled edges of the front and back pieces.

Decorate the house as desired, referring to the photograph for suggestions. Cement staggered rows of shingles, shutters, chimneys, or steps to the house. Draw scallops or crosshatches of icing, squeezing in a steady motion all the way across the house. (You can prevent globs by starting a stream of icing flowing before letting it touch the gin-

gerbread.) Add icicles of icing. Cement a bird, made from a pine cone and feather, on the perch.

GINGERBREAD DOUGH

6 cups (1.2kg) sifted all-purpose flour
4 teaspoons (50g) ground ginger
1½ teaspoons (18.75g) ground cinnamon
1 teaspoon (12.5g) ground cloves
¼ teaspoon (3g) each: ground nutmeg, cardamom, salt
2 sticks (200g) butter or margarine
1 cup (200g) firmly packed light brown sugar
½ cup (125ml) dark corn syrup
½ cup (125ml) light molasses

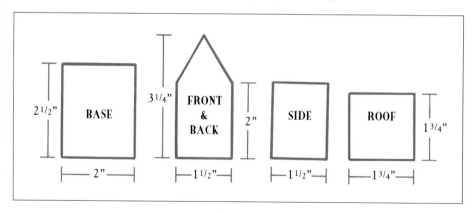

Sift the flour and spices together in a bowl. Combine the butter, brown sugar, corn syrup, and molasses in a saucepan, and stir over low heat until the butter is melted and all ingredients are blended. Remove this mixture from the heat.

Combine a third of the flour mixture with the butter mixture in a large mixing bowl; blend well. Continue adding the rest of the flour mixture, blending until the dough is firm but pliable.

Flour your hands and knead the dough until it is smooth and slightly sticky. If the dough is too moist, add a little more flour, a spoonful at a time. Refrigerate the dough for one hour.

Preheat the oven to 325°F (170°C). Coat two or three cookie sheets with butter and sprinkle them with flour, tapping off any excess. Roll out and cut the dough as indicated in the birdhouse directions. Use a spatula to carefully place dough sections on cookie sheets. Bake until the gingerbread is firm and brown, about twenty to thirty minutes. Let the gingerbread cool completely before assembling the house.

Diminutive Dinosaurs

❀ ❀ ❀

Sweet colors, whimsical patterns, and button pull-toy wheels give these 3" dinosaurs charm and appeal.

MATERIALS:

* Papier-mâché mix
* Matte-finish water-base varnish or sealer
* Acrylic paint in assorted colors
* Four 1/2" sew-through buttons for each dinosaur
* Quilting thread
* Pencil
* Tracing paper
* Rolling pin
* Cellophane wrap
* Cookie sheet
* Craft knife #1

(materials list continues on page 45)

Diminutive Dinosaurs

* Small blunt knitting, darning, or tapestry needle
* Small flat and fine tapered paintbrushes
* Hot-glue gun and hot-melt glue sticks

DIRECTIONS:

Read Using a Hot-Glue Gun and Papier-Mâché on pages 61 and 62. Prepare the papier-mâché and roll it out to about a 3/16" thickness. Trace and cut out the actual-size patterns for each dinosaur (page 69). Use the patterns to cut out a brontosaurus and a stegosaurus.

Referring to the pattern, use a blunt needle to pierce a hole at the top center for a hanging loop and to sculpt some details such as a mouth and a little line at the top corners of each leg. On the stegosaurus, pierce two holes at the base of each triangular plate and sculpt a spadelike shape. Let the shapes dry, then varnish them.

To paint the dinosaurs, add a little white paint to each color to make a sherbet-toned pastel. Using a small flat paintbrush, apply a base coat on both sides, letting the paint dry after each coat. Then use a fine tapered brush and a contrasting color to paint on a pattern of triangles or squiggles. With a quick, up-and-down motion, scatter white polka dots. Add stripes along the edges. Dot the eye with a darker color. Let the paint dry, then repeat on the reverse side.

Hot-glue a button to each side of each leg, positioning the sew-through holes horizontally. Insert a 5" length of quilting thread through the top hole and tie the ends to make a hanging loop.

Woolly Sheep
❆ ❆ ❆

After using these snuggly ewes (4½"×3½") to decorate a tree, combine them with Soft Hearts (page 52) to form a swag—a perfect gift for a newborn baby.

MATERIALS FOR EACH:

* Small amount of ecru polyester fleece fabric
* Small amount of pink or blue cotton fabric

(materials list continues on page 47)

Woolly Sheep

* Sewing thread to match cotton fabric
* Polyester fiberfill
* Black felt-tip marker
* Tiny bell
* 1/8 yard 1/8"-wide satin ribbon
* Fabric glue
* Clamp-type miniature clothespin

DIRECTIONS:

Read Sewing on page 63. Trace the actual-size patterns (page 70) for the sheep's body and head, using them to cut out two body pieces from fleece and two heads from fabric. Also from fleece, cut out a 1/4"×1" strip for a tail. Also from fabric, cut out four 1"×6" strips for legs, and two triangles with 3/4" sides for ears.

Pin the body and head pieces together in matching pairs, and stitch around all but the shortest edges. Clip seam allowances and turn pieces to the right side. Stuff them firmly with fiberfill. Glue the head into the opening of the body.

For eyes, dot the head with a marker. For each ear, fold under two corners on a triangle. Glue or tack the ear to the fleecy part of the head, with the remaining triangle point close to the eye. Tack a bell and a ribbon bow under the head.

For legs, tightly roll each strip and glue it closed. Apply a liberal amount of glue inside the roll and pin the legs under the body until the glue is completely dry. Glue the tail to the rump.

Finish by tacking a miniature clothespin to one side of the ornament for attaching it to a branch of the tree.

Pastoral Angels
✿ ✿ ✿

Follow the directions for the Teddy Bear Quilts (page 50) to create your own patchwork fabric for the dresses of these 4 1/2"-tall angels.

MATERIALS:

* Small amount of muslin fabric
* Small amount of quilted or patchwork fragments
* Ecru sewing thread

(materials list continues on page 49)

Pastoral Angels

* Black and red felt-tip markers
* Red, pink, or orange crayon
* Natural twine
* Polyester fiberfill
* Very slender vine
* Pencil, tracing paper, scissors
* Sewing needle and pins
* Sewing machine (optional)

DIRECTIONS:

Read Sewing on page 63. On tracing paper, trace the actual-size wing pattern (page 71). Mark a circle 2½" in diameter for the head and, referring to the diagram below, a trape-

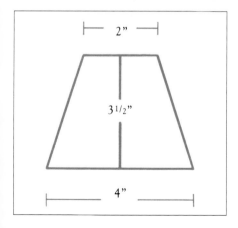

2"

3½"

4"

zoid for the dress. Use the patterns to mark and cut out two heads and four wings from muslin, and two dresses from quilted or patchwork fabric.

Pin and stitch the heads and wings together in matching pairs, leaving the straight edge on the wings and a 1" curve on the head unstitched. Clip into the seam allowances, turn pieces to the right side, and stuff them plumply with fiberfill.

Pin the raw edges of each wing to a side edge of one dress piece, near the top. Place the second dress on top of the first dress, with right sides of the patchwork facing and wings in between. Stitch along all but the top edge. Trim the corners and turn the dress over to the right side. Stuff it plumply. Turn the top edge ¼" to the inside and insert the open edge of the head. Slip-stitch all around the head to secure it.

For the face, use markers to dot eyes and a mouth, crayons to "rouge" cheeks. Tack twine across the top seam, twisting it into curls or ringlets as you go.

For a halo, follow the instructions given in Making a Vine Wreath on page 62 to make a thin ring 1½" in diameter. Tack the halo to the back of the head; leave the thread ends long and tie them together to form a hanging loop.

Teddy Bear Quilts

✳ ✳ ✳

Pose a favorite stuffed toy with one of these patchwork coverlets, 8½" square.

MATERIALS:

* Small amounts of 3 or 4 coordinating cotton print fabrics
* White sewing thread
* 9" square batting
* Four ³⁄₈" sew-through buttons
* Pencil, graph paper, scissors
* Sewing needle and pins
* Sewing machine (optional)
* Iron

DIRECTIONS:

Read Sewing on page 63; refer to the section on making a one-patch or checkerboard patchwork. Follow these instructions to make a 2"-square template (A) and a 1¾"×9" rectangle (B). Use these templates to cut eight A from each of two fabrics for patches; and four B from a third fabric for borders. Arrange the patches into a checkerboard pattern of four-by-four squares. Stitch them into rows, then join the rows together to form a 6½" square.

Add borders. Stitch one border to one side of the patchwork. Trim the border to the same length as the patchwork side. Pin a second border to an adjacent side of the patchwork. Stitch and then trim the extending edge as before. Add a third and fourth border in the same manner.

From any desired fabric, cut a backing the same size as the top of the quilt. Cut the batting ¼" smaller all around. Place the batting on your work surface, then center the backing and the patchwork quilt top, right sides together, on top. Smooth and pin liberally. Stitch around, leaving a 4" opening along the center of one side. Trim the corners and turn the quilt to the right side.

Turn the open edges ¼" to the inside and slip-stitch them closed. Repin the layers together to keep them from shifting. Quilt diagonally across the center of the checkerboard in both directions, then around the border, close to the seam. Sew a button to each corner of the quilt.

Teddy Bear Quilts and Soft Heart

Soft Heart

✳ ✳ ✳

*With a center of potpourri, these 3"
ornaments will add fragrance
to the air during the holidays and are
perfect for tucking into a lingerie
drawer the rest of the year.*

MATERIALS:

* ✳ Large scrap of fabric
* ✳ Sewing thread to match
* ✳ Small amount of polyester fiberfill
* ✳ $1/2$ yard $3/8$"-wide satin ribbon
* ✳ $1/2$" sew-through button
* ✳ 1 tablespoon of potpourri or $1/8$ teaspoon essential oil
* ✳ Sewing needle and pins
* ✳ Pencil, tracing paper, scissors

DIRECTIONS:

Read Sewing on page 63. Complete the actual-size half pattern (page 71); use the pattern to cut out two hearts from fabric.

For a hanging loop, cut a 4" length from ribbon. Fold it crosswise in half and pin it to the right side of one heart, with the loop at the center and the raw edges extending just past the center top edge.

Pin the hearts together, right sides facing. Stitch around, leaving a $1 1/2$" opening along one straight side edge. Clip into the seam allowance and turn the heart to the right side.

Stuff the heart plumply with fiberfill. Make a small well at the center of the heart and push in potpourri or a small ball of fiberfill soaked in essential oil. Complete the stuffing, turn the open edges to the inside, and slip-stitch the opening closed.

Tie a simple bow with the remaining ribbon, and cut each streamer end at an angle. Tack the bow slightly above the center of the heart, securing it with a button stitched on top.

Stocking Instructions

❄

*Christmas stockings are a wonderful place to put special little presents and treats, so
why not make each stocking you create as appealing as the gifts it holds? Try bias stripes of red
pin-dot and muslin to call to mind candy canes and the simple joys of Christmas.
Or a bonus pocket on the front of a stocking to hold a small toy, stuffed animal, or some extra
treats—perhaps even something for the family pet. For a Victorian look, search for the
most sumptuous velvets, jacquards, and trimmings you can find. Or join the humblest fabric
scraps into a country-style patchwork stocking for the littlest angel in your house.*

MATERIALS:

For all Stockings:
* Sewing thread to match fabric
* Sewing machine (optional)
* Sewing needle and pins

For the Victorian Stocking:
* $1/2$ yard each of two complementary fabrics (shown here, printed and solid velvet)
* $1^3/8$ yards narrow gold twisted cord welting
* $1/2$ yard wide gold twisted cord welting
* 1 yard each gold satin cord and tasseled decorator trim

For the Stocking With a Pocket:
* $3/8$ yard reversible quilted fabric

For the Candy-Cane Stocking:
* $5/8$ yard bleached muslin fabric
* $1/4$ yard red pin-dot fabric
* Batting

For Baby's Patchwork Stocking:
* Scraps of assorted printed cotton fabric
* $3/8$ yard gingham or printed cotton fabric
* Batting
* 1 yard $1^1/2$"-wide white eyelet trim

DIRECTIONS:

Read Sewing on page 63.

Prepare the pattern as follows: take the reduced stocking pattern on page 60 to your local photocopy shop and enlarge the pattern at 200% three times, or until the pattern fills an 11"×17" sheet of paper.

Cut out the enlarged pattern. Elongate or shorten the leg of the stocking as indicated or as desired. When cutting out the stocking pieces, be sure to reverse the pattern for the second piece of each pair.

Construct and embellish the stocking according to the following individual directions here and on pages 55 and 60.

For a hanging loop, use a strand of ribbon, or fold a $1^1/2$"×6" strip of fabric lengthwise into thirds. Turn under the long edge of the top third $1/4$" and stitch along that fold. Fold the strip crosswise in half and tack the ends securely inside the top corner of the stocking, on the heel side.

Victorian Stocking:

Extend the leg of the pattern 4". Use the pattern to cut two pieces from each fabric (one for the exterior of the stocking, one for the lining and cuff). Pin the stocking pieces together in matching pairs and sew around all but the top edges.

Sew the welting and tasseled-fringe trims around the top edges of the lining. Turn only the exterior stocking to the right side. Insert the lining. Turn the top edge of the exterior fabric 1/2" to the wrong side and slip-stitch it to the lining.

Turn down a generous amount of cuff, then embellish the corner of the stocking with an extra bow, loops, and tassel-end streamers, tacking everything neatly and securely into place.

Stocking With a Pocket:

Extend the leg of the pattern 4". Use the pattern to cut two stocking pieces from reversible quilted fabric. Pin the stocking pieces together and stitch along all but the top edge.

Make a finished cuff as follows: starting at each top corner and working for 4", trim the seam allowances to 1/8". Turn the stocking to the right side. Turn the top edge forward 1/2" and stitch. Make French seams as follows: keeping the stocking flat, starting at the top corner and working through all layers, stitch 1/4" from the seam for 31/2". Fold this section down.

Scribe a paper circle 10" in diameter, then cut it in half to make a pocket pattern. Use this pattern to cut two pocket pieces from the same fabric as the stocking. Pin the two pieces together, right sides facing, and stitch around the curve. Turn the pocket to the right side. Fold the open edge 1/2" to the wrong side twice and stitch it down. Pleat the front of the pocket until you bring in its width to 6". Stitch across to secure the pleats.

Pin the back of the pocket to the stocking, just under the cuff, and slip-stitch it securely in place all around.

Candy-Cane Stocking:

Prepare the patchwork fabric: for stripes, cut seven 11/2"×18" strips from both the red pin-dot and muslin fabrics. Stitch the strips together along their long edges to form a striped fabric piece that measures 141/2"×18".

Angle the pattern on the striped fabric to cut a stocking piece with diagonal stripes running through it. Also use the pattern to cut three stocking pieces from the muslin

Victorian Stocking

Stocking With a Pocket

Candy-Cane Stocking

Baby's Patchwork Stocking

and two from the batting. Layer the stocking pieces in this order: muslin, batting, striped fabric (right side up), muslin, batting, and muslin. Pin and baste the layers together, keeping edges even. Stitch around all but the top edge. Turn the stocking to the right side.

From the red pin-dot fabric, cut a 2"×14" strip for a binding. Press the long edges 1/2" to the wrong side. Pin the binding along the top edge of the stocking, right sides facing, and stitch 1/2" from the top. Fold the binding over to the inside and slip-stitch the folded edge in place.

Baby's Patchwork Stocking:

Refer to the general instructions on Sewing on page 63 for a one-patch design of squares. Use the square template to cut out a total of thirty-six patches; arrange them in a square as desired. Join them into rows, then stitch the rows together to form a 9 1/2" square. Piece with gingham to obtain a 9 1/2"×17" rectangle.

Place the stocking pattern on the pieced fabric so that the lower part of the stocking features the one-patch design. Also use the pattern to cut two stocking shapes from batting, and three from gingham, for the backing and two lining pieces.

REDUCED PATTERN FOR ALL STOCKINGS

Enlarge this drawing at 200% three times on a photocopier.

For the lining pieces, cut 2"-wide strips from two or three fabrics that were used in the patchwork. Join them and layer them over the top of the lining pieces. Stitch them down, then trim the edges to match the lining pieces.

Layer the stocking pieces in this order: lining (right side down), batting, patchwork (right side up), gingham backing, batting, and lining (right side up).

Pin and baste the layers together, keeping all edges even. Stitch around all but the top edge. Turn the stocking to the right side.

Make a finished cuff, following the directions for the Stocking With a Pocket. Trim the cuff with eyelet trim and add an eyelet bow.

General Instructions
❋ ❋ ❋

The following general instructions are referred to throughout the directions given in this book.

USING A HOT-GLUE GUN

It is important to follow the manufacturer's instructions for your hot-glue gun carefully. Keep a bowl of cold water handy in case of burns. Use tweezers, tongs, or craft sticks (not your bare fingers) to press items into the hot glue. Be sure to unplug the gun when you are not using it, and keep children away from it.

ARRANGING FLORAL MATERIALS

Feel free to substitute materials similar in size and scale to those given in the materials lists. For an effective floral design, establish a focal point such as a large bow, and/or smaller focal points such as ribbon roses or pine cones. All floral materials should enhance these focal points by radiating outward from them along the general contours of the piece. Refer to the photographs for suggestions on how to position items.

MAKING A VINE WREATH

Craft and floral shops usually have grapevine wreaths and wreath forms in many small sizes, although it is easy to make your own. All you need are vines or very slender twigs; honeysuckle and grapevines, and birch and willow twigs work well, as do many others.

If the vines or twigs are still green, they will be pliable enough to work with as is. But if the vines or twigs are too dry and brittle to bend, soak them in water for a few minutes. Then bend them into a ring, measuring for the diameter specified in the individual pattern directions.

To secure the ring, use fine-gauge wire. Continue to wrap the strand of wire around the ring, passing it under and over the original ring and tucking in the ends between pieces. You may start a new piece of twig or vine and keep wrapping to build up the thickness of the ring. Wrap with

wire wherever stray strands need to be held in tightly. Try to cover the wire wrappings by hot-gluing decorative items on top of them.

MAKING A CARDBOARD CONE

Use a compass to mark a circle with a 6" radius on paper. Cut out the circle and fold it in half twice to obtain a quarter-circle wedge. Using this wedge as a pattern, trace and cut out the wedge from cardboard (and wrapping paper, if the cone will be covered). Bring the straight edges of the cardboard wedge together into a cone shape and overlap them by 1/2". Secure the edges of the wedge with masking tape.

To cover the cone, spray the wrong side of the wrapping paper with adhesive. Wait a few minutes until the glue is tacky, then simply wrap the cardboard cone with the wrapping paper.

PAPIER-MÂCHÉ

Prepared papier-mâché mix can be bought at your local art supply store. This clean white cellulose compound combines the best features of clay, plaster, and papier-mâché, and air-dries in about a day.

Trace and cut out the actual-size patterns for each shape shown on pages 65–71. Following the manufacturer's instructions, prepare the papier-mâché. Roll it out on a cookie sheet, striving for a uniform thickness of about 3/8"—lay cellophane wrap on the papier-mâché if you find that it sticks to the rolling pin. Place each pattern on the papier-mâché and cut around the shape with a craft knife. Remove the excess papier-mâché and the pattern.

Referring to the pattern, use a blunt needle to pierce a hole at the top center of the ornament for a hanging loop and to sculpt some details as indicated.

Let the shape dry thoroughly—about twenty-four hours, longer if the air is humid. Seal all surfaces with two coats of water-base varnish or decoupage medium, letting each coat dry thoroughly.

To paint, use a small flat brush. Paint a base coat on one side, let it dry, then paint a base coat on the other side. When dry, use a fine tapered brush to add pattern or details. Let the paint dry, then repeat the pattern on the reverse side. Revarnish if you wish to have a glossy finish.

Insert a 5" length of thread or cord through the top hole and tie the ends to make a hanging loop.

SEWING

You will need small amounts of fabric for most of these projects. If the item will be washed, use prewashed, preshrunk fabric. Tightly woven cottons are often best. Sewing thread should be of a good quality and color-matched or contrasted to the fabric, as desired. Batting should be of the traditional thin variety.

In the individual directions, you are asked to have scissors on hand: it's best to have both fabric-cutting shears and paper-cutting scissors.

Most of the sewing projects can be speedily created with the sewing machine, but you can easily do the sewing by hand.

To make templates for the geometric patches, use a pencil and graph paper. To make patterns for the curved pieces, carefully trace the appropriate pattern onto a sheet of tracing paper.

All templates and patterns include 1/4" seam allowances all around, so you do not have to add them. Cut out the pattern of template and pin it to the fabric, making sure to place the greatest number of straight edges of the tracing along the grain. Lightly trace around the pattern or template with a pencil or a dressmaker's pencil and cut out along these marked outlines.

To sew, pin pieces together with right sides facing and edges even. Stitch 1/4" from raw edges. As you work on pieced items, press the seams to one side.

To create the one-patch or checkerboard patchwork designs, make a 2"-square template. Use the template to cut out the number of fabric squares indicated in the directions. Arrange the squares into a larger square or rectangle, choosing either a checkerboard or random one-patch design. Stitch the squares together into horizontal rows. Press the seams to one side. Sew the rows together, pinning at each intersection of seams to ensure sharp corners. Press the seams flat.

To quilt, you can use either the traditional white thread or the color of your choice. Make a small knot at the end of the thread. Insert the needle from the top surface into the batting so it only re-emerges at the spot where you want to start quilting. Give the thread a small tug to sink the knot into the batting. Make a running stitch, striving for small, evenly spaced stitches. To finish, make a small backstitch.

For ornaments that are to be stuffed with fiberfill, leave an opening for turning. Trim the seam allowance across each corner; clip into the seam allowances at inside angles and along curves. Turn the piece to the right side. Stuff with fiberfill as indicated—lightly, plumply, or firmly. Turn the open edges 1/4" to the inside and slip-stitch them closed.

METRIC CONVERSION TABLE

Compute the conversion, then round off to one number past the decimal point.

1/4" = .635cm
1" = 2.54cm
4" = 10.16cm

1 yard = 91.44cm

Actual-Size Patterns

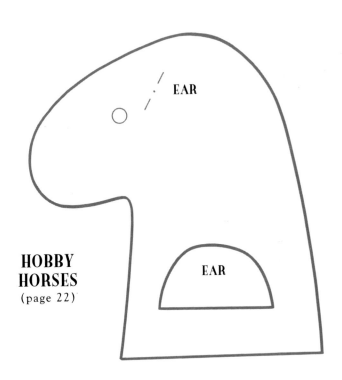

EAR

EAR

**HOBBY
HORSES**
(page 22)

MENAGERIE
(page 29)

FOLK-ART SWAG
(page 33)

68

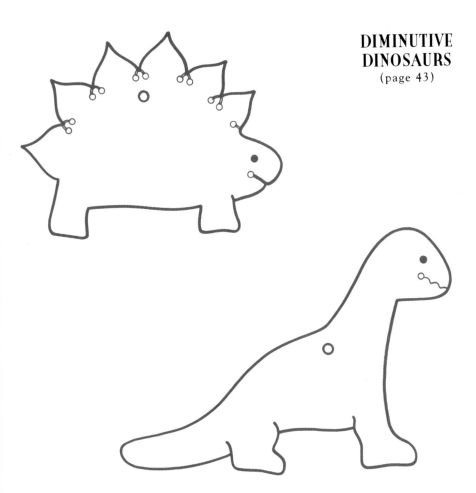

**DIMINUTIVE
DINOSAURS**
(page 43)

WOOLLY SHEEP
(page 45)

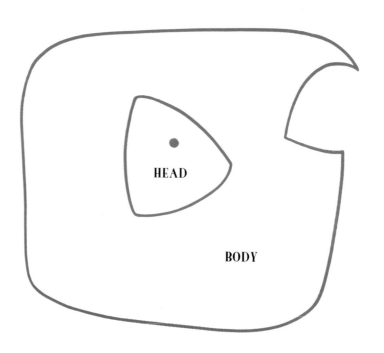

HEAD

BODY

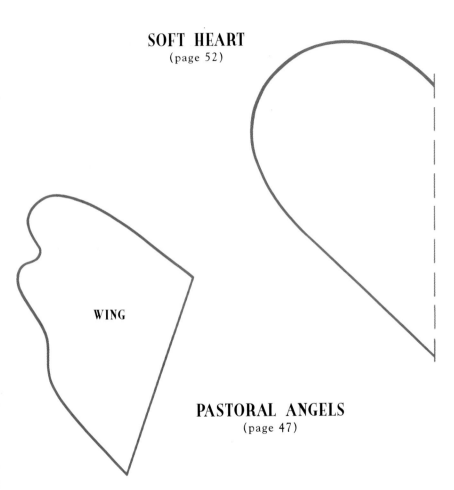

SOFT HEART
(page 52)

WING

PASTORAL ANGELS
(page 47)

INDEX